WHAT BOOKS PRESS

AN IMPRINT OF

THE GLASS TABLE

COLLECTIVE

LOS ANGELES

THE "SHE" SERIES:
A VENICE CORRESPONDENCE

HOLADAY MASON

&

SARAH MACLAY

LOS ANGELES

Copyright © 2016 by Holaday Mason and Sarah Maclay. All rights reserved. Published in the United States by What Books Press, the imprint of the Glass Table Collective, Los Angeles.

Publisher's Cataloging-In-Publication Data

Names: Mason, Holaday. | Maclay, Sarah.

Title: The "She" Series : A Venice Correspondence / Holaday Mason & Sarah Maclay.

Other Titles: Venice Correspondence

Description: Los Angeles : What Books Press, [2016]

Identifiers: ISBN 978-0-9962276-4-3

Subjects: LCSH: Women--Correspondence--Poetry. | Beaches--California--Los Angeles--Poetry. | Los Angeles (Calif.)--Poetry. | American poetry.

Classification: LCC PS3613.A8167 S54 2016 | DDC 811/.6--dc23

Cover art: Gronk, *untitled*, acrylic on canvas, 2015
Book design by Ash Goodwin, ashgood.com

What Books Press
363 South Topanga Canyon Boulevard
Topanga, CA 90290

WHATBOOKSPRESS.COM

THE "SHE" SERIES: A VENICE CORRESPONDENCE

Dedicated, in gratitude, to our mothers—
Barbara Cleo Burrell, Mason, Urschel (4/30/1929–3/20/2011)
Mary Blair Maclay (10/11/1929–6/18/2015)

CONTENTS

⓪

1	HM	"The book is still..."	16
	SM	"Insect days..."	18
2	HM	"Sound out the room..."	20
	SM	"Time spun in the midst of antlers..."	22
3	HM	"She emerges wet..."	24
	SM	"Begin with *peignoir*..."	26
4	HM	"He said, 'It was a zoo...."	27
	SM	—as, *after Odysseus, her body wanted to be Ophelia*	29
5	HM	"She walks (as I watch)..."	31
	SM	"Night had snuffed out its own stars..."	33
6	HM	"Neck, held back in a bow..."	35
	SM	—*Valentine's Day*	37
7	HM	"Now to revisit the hill afterwards..."	38
	SM	"Because identity had gone..."	39

⓪⓪

8	HM	"The answer is no, regarding the key..."	44
	SM	"She had *wanted* to say: something about the night yard..."	45
9	HM	"There was a phone call and a hang-up..."	46
	SM	"Or Mrs. Bovary's growing addiction to fabric..."	47
10	HM	"The winter inside the afternoon..."	48
	SM	"It's questionable: whether there is a 'she'..."	50

11	HM	"*Consider the wings of certain rare* . . ."	51
	SM	"*The butterfly wings are broken* . . ."	52
12	HM	"A single bell . . ."	53
	SM	"The night did not end in pewter . . ."	55
13	HM	"With a care just the other side of reverence . . ."	57
	SM	"It's a deep red saddle . . ."	58
14	HM	"Again, birds. Birds again . . ."	59
	SM	"Dawn blooms like a memory . . ."	60
15	HM	"She sees obsidian . . ."	61
	SM	"And I imagine her lying there . . ."	63
16	HM	"At the 23rd floor pane, a raven. . ."	64
	SM	"There had been the glass of Pernod . . ."	66
17	HM	"The hair had to be cut . . ."	68
	SM	"And after, she walks quickly past the skaters..."	70
18	HM	"& all the while—there are liquid currents of open air . . ."	72
	SM	"Travel had been a kind of mourning . . ."	74

⓪ ⓪ ⓪

19	HM	"*pause* / Gargantuan twinkle . . ."	78
	SM	"Deep in the woods . . ."	80
20	HM	"So I was sitting there . . ."	82
	SM	"Without remembering exactly when . . ."	83
21	HM	"She is BOLD as toast . . ."	84
	SM	"They smell her . . ."	86
22	HM	"She finally arrived (after having been nearly forgotten) . . ."	87
	SM	"She had learned to speak to the ones who were already . . . ."	88
23	HM	"'Make my grave shallow so I can feel . . .'"	89
	SM	"(It had been a rainbow of waves: . . ."	90
24	HM	"What waltzed up the alley that night . . ."	91
	SM	"The man, you see, was expressing, was pressing . . ."	95
25	HM	"Such talk, such rabble . . ."	96
	SM	"So we went on the velvet journey of his voice . . ."	98
26	HM	"'It's deserted,' she says . . ."	100
	SM	"(At the center of this was a dream . . ."	101

27 HM	"While going up, she asks . . ."	102
SM	"Here is your mirror, because you can't see . . ."	103
28 HM	"Twice now she's been blinded . . ."	104
SM	"There was her method of swooning . . ."	106

① ① ① ①

29 HM	"It's Thanksgiving . . ."	110
SM	"But there was another subject . . ."	112
30 HM	"It happens when we're very tired . . ."	113
SM	"Strands of sirens and crows . . ."	114
31 HM	"Twisting, we smell of wet horses/salt/granite . . ."	115
SM	—*Mystery Box*	116
32 HM	"I took you inside . . ."	118
SM	"The dark space was now in a gully—a kind of hollow—"	119
33 HM	"There was no handbook . . ."	120
SM	"If it occurs in a room . . ."	121
34 HM	"There are changes in her features . . ."	123
SM	—*November, after the Jeffers Fest*	124
35 HM	"The brightness of March daffodils shook his nervous system . . ."	126
SM	"If the presence in the hallway . . ."	127
36 HM	"I am dancing, not quite falling . . ."	130
SM	"*Necessaire*: albedo . . ."	132
37 HM	"Maybe it was snow he dreamed of . . ."	133
SM	"It was just a field . . ."	135

Notes	140
Acknowledgements	142

Her body thus became a medium for the representation of curious and momentary phenomena that partly dissolved forms and offered to the observer the gay and capricious spectacle of dancing light.
—John Rewald, *The Impressionist Brush*

1   HM

The book is still, is closed, so

casts a square shade on the woman's knee
where she kneels at the pond, & still the sorting goes

on—

The book is open, is a question about waiting—

the kiss planted,
want now saturated with a pale cool sheen.

Not knowing any longer—what's behind, what's before,

the woman above & the one below, both
lean & touch mouth to mouth, intently considering

The Face

in the still clear surface, while way up & beyond, vapors of clouds

shape her

hair into white tufting Antoinette coils, the head, a head in clouds
& not in the blood or in the garbage, in the blood or the want.

The pages flutter open.
There is a body lying still.

The body is the mother, my mother.
I spread open her ribs &
count them gently

until they lute & harp / violet glands now fruits & veins steaming
with tenderness. Your mother's here too.

Men will come with boats soon.

It was just a book.
It was a painting in a museum of a woman with a book.

There was a shimmering pool & a world.

1   SM

Insect days. At night, the pure dilemma
of the moon.

Here is my answer: obsidian lacquer.
Here is my answer: paint the moon black.

Give me time to re-align
my "practices and habits"

—by recognizing them.
He said. She said.

(At this point they tossed their velvet
voices in the trash.)

Talk to me like dirt.
Talk to me like wind.

Talk to me like sweat.
Use your plainest voice.

Walk with me into this new room.
Light a match, if you must see.

Do not pretend you have to name it,
limit it or know it.

Call this a riddle.
Let the room speak.

Call this permission.
Call this a prayer.

Do not say I do not love
the moon.

2   HM

Sound out the room—
this breast & altar.
It is fugue.
You say I have the eyes of an owl.

We remember
deliverance in hips
tasting of rust & sugar.
This is my brow. This is your pelvis.

Not reluctant to spill,
I know how much loneliness weighs.
But we can't talk to everyone. Night
just forgets the shapes of skyscrapers

& wind never forgets anything.
So easy, pilgrim, I can mill, bite.
It's my honor, not a habit,
this slow unraveling of my yellow skirt.

Put what's been whispered into you
back inside of me. (Careful.)
Red is slippery with time &

there is some word I'm looking for, so costly.
I might ask . . .
how long is God's breath—the extract
of thunder,

the trance—the entrance of the eyes?
I opened.
You were named.
No jeopardy or repeating, ever.

Three clay-colored turtledoves land inside my palm,
cooing & whispering & I remember
everything.
I'm alone.

It is Christmas.
Breathe.
I will always love
wild horses.

2   SM

Time spun in the midst of antlers
        and guns. It was hung with pine—
                cones suspended from time

symmetrically, like icicles. Time itself
        was surrounded by leaves, was draped
                with a saddle, and horns. Above it,

the head of a deer. Above it,
        on a tiny balcony in sudden color,
                a general—and a fraulein, or queen—

in white, in red, in black. The balcony
        pleated like a skirt. The fraulein's skirt
                un-pleated. Time

wanted to beat its wings, but had none.
        Had, instead, a couple of arrows,
                pointing at numbers. Time was caught

in a circle, but not for long.
        The circle lay against a piece of wood,
                and even that wood was a record

of longer time. One only had to look.
        Time was surrounded
                by a rabbit and an early conquistador

in knickers and a blunderbuss, but above
        the spinning of time, even the stocks
                of the guns, before our eyes,

were turning into birds.
        And the birds began to fly.

3   HM

she returns to the surface   silk black
nipple   feet   fingers   nails   emerges spine
past   belly   forward —no—stop—   half
now-half then   black metal   half no   half yes
closed eyes   o black   the perfect mouth   no sound
no vowel   & still   she emerges   new   wet
orchid   chisel   window

he is farther out
penis   yes cock yes   fish   and
still undisturbed by being   (yes
& no)   now   (always & never)   come   into   the smooth metal
night   into light   half cast   fingers of tar
gleaming oil   He is coming—tar & skin   now
he moves into "The Story"   He is coming   into
the narrative   *(and of course on top resides the star.*
Full of always/never. Full grown, the man emerges and begins
running hard into her. Inside her it all begins.)

She is a   black moon   perfect starless
night   perfect hidden teeth she is
pensive now &   yes coming owl,
out into time then   —no—stop—no
sinking back into   stone & soot
ash & obsidian (snake/wind)   she is the She
a skillet of cells   afraid/unafraid   & the back of the moon   a pattern
of music   seasons   small coiling animals
some with wings   *(she is not on top so clings to him*
with her two legs and also hands and also mouth until
She finds vowels, consonants—a string of light—new leaves
shimmering—and they become . . .) emerge.

Now—yes now   come into—the story
from the never   two shadows   your spine & jaw   rib
come   toward me, away from   nothing is
dense as iron   Now   you   emerge into
this now   —listen   the cock   the fish   the
cicada   the leaf —   the soft tissue   hand to mouth   all
emerge—   where   all   will   become
wrecked & torn   until another—   yet still things come & come
in color   & it is wet   where before   it   just was

3   SM

Begin with *peignoir* and end with a rustle of iris, along the edges. Begin with the sea but sublime into a body, swimming in purple. Begin with that matter of itching; end with that matter of arousal. Do not concern yourself with form, or fear. Begin with forgetting but end as an orchid, slick as squid ink, mirror of mouth. Let the photographers track your swelling; equally, your health. Begin as crystal; end as fluid. Start with discord; end with chord. No one will tell you, before, that you will feel, acutely, color. Say "violet." Say "warmth." Begin with salt.

4   HM

He said, "It was a zoo"—

out there, in the lucid pre-dawn sea
where Ophelia sang all sorts of animals towards the surface

until they touched his thighs,

slid over & under, became skin to his skin.

The walrus arrived—still vibrating urchin flowers
& sunlight even before sun had come—

lavender dolphins, purple skimmers, licks of fin, slid, twisted—
the quartz & tourmaline pelicans groaned

near a graphite cusp of sky

sewn with white seagulls, beneath which whales
breached blue as ripe plums

& fish & fish & fish & spears of minnows.

A man in the sea is in the drum of the world,

his buried sadness wavering
overhead as if all

stitches were healed, bone fragments healed, eruptions of longing

forgotten onshore, sealed tight & away.

A man firm inside a woman lies under the hexagon spell of starlight.
He enters the salt inside her—begins to need salt.

This is how a man comes to prefer

living alone—his body changed into ocean—

the moon in its reflection, a compass steering him to disappear—

This is the way opposite things can be sometimes, when they touch.

4 SM

—as, after Odysseus, her body wanted to be Ophelia

The pistol came with its own music.

An echo slid from her throat:

Liquid, alive beyond common names for color.

How at night she could not swim.

Her song like a line of neon in wavering slices

across the crinoline dark

until the dogs began to bay

and men slipped into the skins of animals

to roll against the mud without the barrier of clothes.

How that bay was a living jewel—the sound, the topaz water—

the water had poured from her

and become alive.

She would wash up on the shore or float,

as white as the lizard who pulls the carriage

in a dream, all soggy finery

and hair and reeds.

Over and over

her body was painted

in darkness,

like a wine of skin.

What was true:

It was up to her to invent

her own music,

as she began to hear it

in the growing stain of sky.

5   HM

She walks (as I watch)

slowly backwards the quarter mile from the low tide shoreline
& then, more slowly still,

each step up the cement staircase,

unable to face forward & fully leave her lover.

A streetlamp blows out.
The Ferris wheel now
fuchsia, then
turquoise, now
emerald, then
gold.

The razor of the sunset bleeds into the sea also,

disappearing towards the whips
of curled wind, what forces leaf litter
up through the licorice red twist of the horizontal sphere—

(My spine is beaded mercury)

The lover left behind plays his plain guitar, a cycle, the cut of moon

while black gulls suspend
over his back like many hands—

(my hair, medusa-born, sparks into circles).

Three things fall over at the highway—
(maybe trash cans tumbling into the intersection) & cars swerve hard.

The flurry of white butterflies
unwinds from a nest in the gust-shredding palms,

all kindling in a dark canyon—that which has not yet burned

but will soon.

5   SM

Night had snuffed out its own stars—
even deep in the country.

The porch light was on, a little harsh,
against this backdrop of nothing.

You could see the two of them
talking—earnestly. And pondering,

his eyes the color of *People Magazine*.
Her thought poured into her mouth—

a slight snag twisted it. Their friends
had taken to constant marketing—

of themselves. He could barely drive
for the over-stimulation. Time had been

disabled, momentarily.
What he would remember most about her

was the look on her face—the way
thought stopped her face from flowing,

knotted it—
that and the look of her shins,

almost shiny in the night air,
like the underbelly of a fish—

a trout, coming up from the cold lake
water, glistening in the dark wind.

6   HM

Neck, held back in a bow. Lamb given to the knife. He whispered into her ear from behind,

"slippery like a fish."

Sitting on the edge of the claw

foot-tub, she reflects on her Self in the window, in the cradle of candle lit night / the door, way behind black—so thirsty. A cup of bath water where both feet float like fish. She is nearly old but not quite too old.

Having nothing to do with the need. Having everything to do with need (touch/torch/bellies).

He asks her to turn off the lights.

Having nothing to do with anything less than fear. Her face in the window, what is under the water & rising to the surface, the way one can barely make out a ghost or a fish.

Bending hard, as if he hated her or perhaps envied the flexible bow of her back, so pliant—a sail full of snow breath. Or as he recalled the bow & arrow story

& would always be the prince.

Pinned as any butterfly to the canvas of the bed, yet "slippery, like water" (

When I was a girl . . .)—the enormous size of his hand at her throat & the tongue of sorrow just behind her

lips unexpressed & in the throat as well.

Torn flags—the palms bending in a high wind of canal. Flames—the light of the neighbor's bathroom flicked on, casting her upturned face in it.

& the neighbor then peeing in his bowl (

I begin again. As a girl I had a long patience for getting the difficult fruit of pomegranates . . .) What a pity it must be for the man not to love the woman with

his beautiful penis.

What a pity . . . as they forget

into each other, each other & themselves.

6   SM

—Valentine's Day

White chicken
Attached to a tree
At neck and legs
With string

7   HM

Now to revisit the hill afterwards—
the wet grass—

the place of surrender

where what is "his" becomes, in tandem, "mine."

I wanted just to lie down all night on the grass,

body in between—

soil, sky, skin, water, water, water, water,

white months of starlight
disintegrating within & over me, velvet
re-collected in small furious pulses,
long hours of indigo

soaked into bone—hips:
thunder, the waking trees & red, red birds, rain too, slight &
precise as scissors.

7 SM

Because identity had gone

        And no one was waiting

(There was no garden, no stair,

There was no snow)—

        Someone, for instance,

Would not be able to hear

        Callas whisper

All the familiar objects

        Had been removed

There was the sound of traffic—

        But in the morning of a foreign city

Under the upturned corners

        Of the mouth

What was there

                        When the muscles went

Why would no one

                        Speak about it

It was not a dilemma

                        But a state

Air was moving

                        Through the scarves of women

Seen from the bus—

                        Through cypress,

                                    Eucalyptus

People held their clothing on,

                        Tightly

It was hard to know

                      What to hear

Was a film already empty

                      The script had been written

The sound of birds

                      Infiltrated me

A huge, swaying texture

                      Like Beethoven

Soaring out of the Schönbrunn

                      A moving curtain surrounding the windows

In and out of sleep

                      Walking silently through trees

8   HM

(The answer is no, regarding the key she wears around her neck, which swings just above the alabaster of her cold belly, an unopened cork in a bottle which, without breathing, will coil.

Thursday & the preemptive sigh
of the front door closing, another pure mini-saga of cost reporting—

it's not good enough to be vigilant; one must act accordingly.)

8   SM

She had *wanted* to say: something about the night yard full of its white flowers (Vita's or Vanessa's, she could no longer recall),

but when she looked again they were candles—a yard of white candles—lit, incandescent, luminous.
                       And, she had to admit, that thing on her leg
was refusing to heal.

Lace—she had thought she'd begin—or some other word with an "l"—lord, lard.

These are the sounds like plates, like petals of rounded, falling white.

(And that this was a kind of gesture—)

9   HM

There was a phone call & a hang-up but a message floated around her head

as
if

she'd grown a cape of long filly hair while the traffic light changed.

It seems there is a little lacquered spring in the air—

said the light.

This set her to wondering about tools of purpose:
what is a turquoise velvet dress, anyhow, if not
a sort of sliver or slide show representing apex, what floats over—
an ocean on a woman's body & what about
the coffee rituals of early risers, after many thoughtful nights, or
the flicker of a green arrow in her eyes (repeat & spin)—.

a very good time

(poof).

9   SM

Or Mrs. Bovary's growing addiction to fabric:

Adopt a title instead of a name—
all else follows.

Mrs. Bovary: title plus "*sur*" name of someone else—
"name" "above" a name.

Back-end linkage to some family dynasty
or other, plug-in to the vertical, over time.

Where does "Emma" go, then?

(Like a secret password, such as "token"—)

Meanwhile, all we really have
is the daily horizon.

It does not occur to me, at first, what the tapping is—
the tapping we call "rain."

I don't recognize my headache
as a kind of hunger.

10   HM

The winter inside the afternoon slipped back into the afternoon
recalling the lateness, the passage of hours.

She did not really wish for an end to life, just to pain, which otherwise
seemed implausible.

(Claim. Clamor, chemise, calm—the proper temper of a woman as reflected in
advertising & the standard of eternal beauty.)

The promise of the floating white flowers was told to her & remained— but
perhaps as shroud, or rest, or fresh snow & so, as a result, she often lit candles

to keep the darkness off her shoulders.

The "I" that created the "she" was keeping her distance, but not really.
There were the particulars

of a stained tea cup, the trees which kept dropping some slippery seeds all over
the porch outside the front door.

Some struck her arms, one her cheek, she turned it the other way, of course—
but slipping, slippage, silage, sadness, all too possible, what with

the loss of history & heritage—the "I" losing her farther eyesight, while
the "she" had bouts of sleeplessness & cowboys

still threatened in bars to kill each other with a single bullet,
& Russian royalty stopped writing poems, going instead for a better showing

on the canvas of the world—making bad movies & bad football.
It had been a brutal year of following the wrong music.

10   SM

It's questionable: whether there is a "she"—a "she" with her heart full of bees.

But there are eyes that tame them.

And then they lift—the bees of assumption—disperse, like clouds, a soft marine layer reflecting heat, a butterscotch heat and, therefore, tangerine as well as gray

until no bees, but ants—so tiny they're almost specks of dirt, as though survival has required a sudden further miniaturization—

as she floats, stunned at her floating, above the jets, the bubbles, within the womb of the pool, the heat—she floats like a large green leaf, soggy and limp

enough that one could remove her with the twist of a stick—
her body would follow

(as ants spill over the edge with the sleepy un-grasp of her hand—)

11   HM

Consider the wings of certain rare butterflies, she says—*& how we vanish.*

The question really is: whether or not he will get lost & lose his head—
or will he lick from the rim, as if kick-box training, will he tough it out

& reach to touch the emerald fold, the elegant watery gap
before
it dissolves back into the vastness—

It burns, he says.

I know—she whispers & leans closer—*one can justify
any belief, even none.*

11 SM

The butterfly wings are broken. She said.
Then we must fix them. He said.

12   HM

        A single bell
spun at its center.

There was no one there.
The dawn

was a puzzle
in pewter hush—
        small whispers, increments

seeping in, like a tea ceremony.

When she placed her tender
foot to the earth,

it was supple, velvet.

When she raised her eyes,
        the world was hung

        in white crystal—wet sighs.
It seemed to be this that aroused the murder

of crows, but even they were subdued & graceful.
Breadfruit, lemons, crooked
half-formed oranges uncorked
        & seemed to twist in joy.

And when it was warmer,
before the people

began to come outside,
she saw the many

parts of prayers still dissolving
into the moss & the un-bloomed trees were strewn

with the branches of other trees

in the fondest embrace.

12   SM

The night did not end in pewter
                              but in a patter
of rain,
         slipshod
                       over the skylights
and dim light.

Here was a way to tell the events
                              of the evening
if one removed the rugs:

Essentially, the couches were false
              (if comforting)

                    without pattern—

and pattern, established,
repeated—

[here is where it burst]

the overlay

of the lie of simple
                              uniformity—

of color, texture,
expectation,
                    match.
                                    Pattern
on pattern, on pattern: this was the way.

                            The rain
in and out
            in its silver.

Silver beyond the metaphor

of tears—

13   HM

With a care just the other side of reverence she slit it open & peeled the rind from the fruit with her fingers. Not a single one of the multitudes of black satin seeds, coal dark wet pearls, containing many old minutes & a great deal of residual salt & music, slipped

through her hands.

The taste was of monarchs. He watched her squatting, rocking back & forth on her heels as she ate very slowly. The moon rose, not over a fire he had rubbed from wood, but over her naked shoulders. The inky waters beyond were on fire with twisting fish, as if the moon

swam in the waters.

What is it to suck the flesh of the sun? He watched her extremely closely but not rudely, while continuing to smile, more & more deeply, inside. They long ago had lost their hats. Papaya was dripping down her arms, turning her

into a tree.

13 SM

It's a deep red saddle—
leather, thin & worn.

I like the way,
he says, *you were playing with time.*

The chair is rocking slightly as the lolli
finds its dollop, licks.

It's a deep red—supple,
thin & warm.

Are you in there? he said.
I am, she said. *I'm here.*

(The face they were looking for
was no longer the one they could see.

And, also, there was blood
but this was part of a pattern.)

14   HM

Again birds. Birds again

were flying

into the windows.

Signal thump.
The magnetic pull,

the wooly threads

of her blood aroused them,

Finally she opened
the silver box which had been sent
months ago

(silver, overused but
still redeemable in most countries).

Inside were several layers of pale green tulle
rolled into tight balls

as if for some game.

14   SM

Dawn blooms like a memory—
gray tree bark and fur

of deer—dun-colored camouflage
for mud and fog.

The morning veers
inward.

Silver has no currency.
Only hush.

The airport is deserted.

The ghosts of brightness vanish
into cars across a street.

An Asian man whose home I may have stayed in
many years ago

sits silently across the vacant aisle of a train,

carrying a silver shopping bag,
one piece of luggage.

Snow is memory.

And the city,
sleep.

15   HM

She sees the obsidian. *Seriously—*

you can't really be afraid of the re-arranged height, no I mean, light, he says
& offers lemon,
yes,

pure lemon cake before
guiding her   through

the almost-freezing expanded bright hallways of mirrors
        to the past & into, also,
        the dreams of the mad—
        those
        glaring portraits of the velveteen desert,
        a perfect moon cooling the low-slung spine
        of the singing lion,
        his peaceful breath   a storm.

He leads her hand over
the city.
She observes her hand over
the city
like a finger on a jeweled button (the city)
        & in the palm of his other hand—a stolen marriage bed.

Whistling way down below
in the streets, in the canyons between buildings

(*afraid of heights? You can't see, seriously…? The black-crayon twirling descent of potency?*)

she watches the world/no, really, just a single congested street—
so small at the tip

of her boot, which is at the fantastic ledge of the building—
the people, like insects & pebbles,

seem to be all in black & every one without their genitals
& also, she thinks, *without the moon,*
without collar bones
& without the

halo (hallow) moon.

15   SM

And I imagined her lying there, alone, in the cathedral, nearly invisible, in the late light of the afternoon, listening to the mad keys of the organist and his kind hair, strewn, streaming across the enlivened air in a kind of mass of curl—and this is wrong—air, hair, wet hair, wet from the playing, as she lay there, lay there before being discovered—and dismissed. She had loved the trees—the metal trees—of Madison Park, and the metal boulder—thought them beautiful—which I only saw at night. But they were terrifying—I thought of my brother, making them, as he could have, welding them together. Tin woods in a forest-park of fall-plucked trees, like an omen: only *metal* trees—furious, arguing, held together in their mutually branching dance of rage. Siamese trees. And, beyond them, blue light of the Empire State—and the gold, triangular tower—shorter, closer; far behind us now, churches with names like Grace; the Chrysler with its lights—isolated in their knife-like spire—white light flung like broken piano keys.

16   HM

At the 23rd floor pane a raven screeches,

circles, nearly cross-eyed,
its metallic gaze wacked & hot & so, seemingly

far above the hot

pink Gerber daisies, cut short & stuck in a squat drinking
glass on the hotel table which she has pulled close to view the huge
downtown panorama.

What she bought today
in the market
(near the lamb-seller's stand at the corner of 6th Ave. & Broadway)
were these flowers & some punished strawberries—

the ruined hidden for obvious reasons
under the beautiful, the perfect ripe ones.

We do not take our "selves" into public

she thinks, sitting there nude under her too-large clandestine
coat, "her" black scarf, under her
flapping navigator's hat.

Now in the liminal cold—the park is indeed central,

each copper rooftop of the city skyline lancing the cerulean sky.
Indicative:

this the invention of subordination—

what is "mine" is "his," is not "ours," is not of an un-punctuated sky.

They sell real fur coats cheap & her wrists are poor with poor versions of roses
sprayed on in Sacks.

The clarified trees listen. The human:
vertical/vertigo/vain/rough/illiterate shove. The men here

are covered. Men everywhere are covered.

Trains like
streams of blood go down towards the river.

16   SM

There had been the glass of Pernod, clear as urine.
She had nearly forgotten to pour in the water, forgotten
        to make it milk and cloud.
                      And so, citron-yellow,
  it was shared.

She sat at the table. His fingers were long
                and he wore leather bracelets
around his neck, or around his wrists
                    as the friend,
all raspberry-orange, appeared at the table,
                        suddenly:

standing just to the side of the slim white linen.

(Of course, one would think one could tell them apart,
                          by the hair . . .)

Meanwhile, she bit and licked her lips to hide
                the chapping, pulling from winter.

Even with the chapping
        and the gesture on display,

on the landing, before they entered the room with the paintings—
        that is, of course, with the Freud—
he finished his story about the house—
                the mirror had dropped
from the wall after hanging for fifteen years;
                     had shattered
across the floor as he sat on the couch, speaking
to his sister
        (should he buy the brownstone
                  (clearly, yes))—
and put a finger toward his lips
to suggest a space, a hush—
              and so it was.

And there were men she nearly introduced to him
in the museum shop—

            men who turned their heads
and didn't answer to their names.

17   HM

The hair had to be cut. Had become

untamable & shivering.
The years were always the middle of life

for someone. She & the furniture were rearranged

in every damned hotel room.
Well-spent time,

deep & well. What people take the witch to,
the water-witch, which scurries in search of deep water.

She did not forget this even when faced with a harsh outcome.

She has a call or is the call & calls & calls & he
is a whisper of black crossed-ripped scars over the sternum,

the low chakra—but no—that is later—
she is ahead of herself
or someone is.

REGARDLESS:
He has effect.
He reads the line of the horizon.
He is counting on the crop of clouds.
It is before the gunmetal of the war splatters on the clouds.
It is before the huge-eyed moth weeps or splashes its wing-dust against that which is
Already Fact.

The hair could not grow beyond that point.

17   SM

And after, she walks past the skaters, into another past—
a blond one, yes, and gently, yes, over another repast

in darkened booths near ice, beside suspended tiny light
and figures etching figure eights, the silver clank of silver

and the clink of glass and after, long after the long spring
nights above Plum Creek and the radio announcing

something, over and over, about Slade Gorton, "in the back room,"
as votes were counted and a distant November

ushered in a change of guard in the small room of a wooden-floored
apartment in Seattle and after the marriages on separate coasts

and her miraculous and kind
divorce and his becoming not a father exactly,

but a kind of grandfather

and after remembering how her lover had been his lover's lover
and his lover (etching a figure eight) had become the lover of her friend

in another decade

(oh, how the blue silk shadows brought this tangibly to mind)—
a simple acceptance, a splash of water, *salut!*

—a little wine, some meat—
the only war at a cloudless distance

of two hundred years or more
before—a distance begging:

reconsider. Just reconsider
the facts.

They had been lovers.
Now they were "history."

So he wrote history.
Never mind

the contents of the meal: time,
like the gold infinity circles

outside, in the cold.

18   HM

& all the while

        there are liquid currents of open air—
        ordinary eddies flaming/fired (lit) with tissue & minerals,
        heavy with colorful (gemstone) curative properties—
        & the moon (a magnet) & the closer stars— naked.

In lock step, domestic & furtive beasts have habits of waking just as she begins

        to sleep

& oh yes, recalls the rejecting "lover"—
he (royal, flaxen rope) was always *over there* enjoying the "view," staying high up
        close to power
& at a distance from need—(to reside inside her, to taste her) the glamour
of every city rising in pale fog beyond the black water—
        A smashed plum
        & oh, those

brilliant shadows of pleasure (the kiss, the meat)— the factual gauntlet only
        her residual pooling memory.

        She'd just used him as imago (at the edge) to guard against (azure)
        exactly this,
        exactly *this* understanding—
that it's possible to love only when the executioner's blade is kissed & one
        is weaned of
            the story (the meat).

(*And this is not a dream.*) Cesarean (blade).

One might decide "misanthrope" is an adjective or verb & not a noun.
Over, now what was it... the course of the fourth winter alone, she understood
    (power) the witch (herbal),the Hag (spool) as she lived in Los Angeles
    with its dry riverbed, its unbroken maidenhead-starless-ness

    & high voltage streetlights—this, without irony (narcissus).

Understood too, something of futility— the human skin was always marbled silt
    & shiny ash (dark music),
    some language of pure impression (oiled god)— a fingerprint perhaps
    of the spirit in a fit of lust—these dark shadows covering our bodies are
    the slow slant of a lowering eyelid.

    Then she hears footsteps across the west (stamina), *then slower*
    across the porch (chalice) *before they stop* (within her).

The reward is to watch (simple) (torture) (golden grain)
    what begins after this, after all of this is finished.

18   SM

Travel had been a kind of mourning.
But now it was over. The gray cat lay on the bed like a fur.
The fountain was full, but not falling. Her smell
was sour and brown.

All is fragmented, correctly. All.

The house looks like a set
belonging to dead people.
The era isn't clear.

A slice of blood orange
lies on the concrete floor
like a leaf, the peel
scraped clean by teeth.

Ants come.

19   HM

pause

Gargantuan twinkle of grassy eyes (before the glasses) as she squeezes the creamy cream, cream from the still tightly-wrapped Twinkies on the shelf in the third row from the meat section of the Vons while another woman, a stranger, watches & enjoys this.

pause

Now, from her position on her back, staring into the water-stained dropped ceiling penetrated with reverse stars, she arranges her body so the fire sprinkler's a bull's-eye over her forehead, & she likes, awfully well, the possibility of a light rain inside the room, watering her third eye, while her green (grassy knoll) eyes, by necessity, close. A light bulb bursts in the shim dance cast off the tiffany lamp & not inside her head—it just happens to go dim at that moment—blink. Whatever happens in her mind is in her mind. What? Blink.

change

Two years earlier, when she'd said with her English eyes (& some words
of course, but now she lies about that part), with her fire green eyes, she'd
passionately said to the foreign person (or something like that) that she could,
maybe, LOVE him—actually—to which he said words which were impressively
unintelligible & in a very high frequency that hurt a lot—
clearly the opposite of "hello" & "fertile."

volume up(voluminous sugar).

Under the bullhorn sun there've been many world wars & deaths by lack of love
& also by

fire.

19   SM

Deep in the woods, within earshot of secrets, we sat on a tree.

We sat in the woods, within earshot of secrets.

We sat on a tree—carved out, like a bench.

There, the blue around the photo was less blue.

Right next to the photo, there was a mark

that looked like a name—but may have been a (simple) discoloration.

It was a short name, short enough to have been an error.

The more I looked at it, the less I could tell.

The night that lived in his house looked the same in the day.

You could drive by and see the streaks on the windows against the black.

In the woods, within earshot of secrets, we sat on a tree—carved out, like a bench.

If he had moved out, night had moved in.

Young men had walked by with their tubas, encased clarinets,

stealing food from the table.

It created a space, barely visible, in which a lighter blue—

There was no need for curtains.

Such as we were. We sat on a tree.

Then he said, "fuck 'em," and kissed me.

The house was not abandoned:

the house was full of night.

His car, for instance, never moved.

His car, for instance, stayed.

20   HM

So I was sitting there & thought it best to break into her house.
So I broke into her house because I was sitting there & this was all about chocolate anyhow, whatever "they" say about the uses of boiling water & red-eye flights, forget that now, I broke in & propped the door open with a sticky dog-bone, & promptly broke four, maybe five of her ice-crystal hangers, the ones she used to put fire away for the night. Of course, she had no broom (I'm the one with the broom) & fire is flighty stuff, vampy & particular, given to fits of flirting & ever so snotty about the scent of dog teeth on bone . . . which is another tale. Regardless, I'm sitting there thinking about the shattered ice when fire got out & ran circles around the cement basketball court, the one right beside the silent flat platinum sea—what is interesting here however is not the sea, but the fact that the men playing ball saw absolutely nothing, I mean nada, even though fire wears heels as high as a volcano sprouting all manner of ripe fruit & full blooming flowers, & is, well, as you can imagine… pretty hot. This is about the time I realize I've run off after a fire, leaving the door ajar & no broom to clear the broken lot of shimmering icy glass & water is (pretty insidious, jealous, in fact) starting to boil over on the stove—so I just sit down to watch the game (not too good, by the way) because after all it was such a relief the wind had knocked all the trees back into a proper line-up & street lamps had returned to their mumbling tasks & the tranced-out fat women polishing the hidden gnomes snapped out of it & got back to their proper job of throwing graffiti from airplane windows, so water & fire could duke it out on their own—they had plenty of experience, & I could go back to whatever I was doing before all this started which, as I was sitting there, occurred to me—must have had something to do with chocolate.

20 SM

Without remembering exactly when, I knew she had described (or was about to) a woman whose hair would resemble a hive—I imagined it sleekly pulled back and up from the center, held a little tight by pins invisible to the eye, could see her sea green eyes, a nose a little wobbled on one side, no make-up—very large hair. The woman seemed as brash as a parrot. Vibrant—yet, a stranger. That is, a woman known only from the outside. It was peculiar to imagine her as a neighborhood fixture—like, I suppose, a street lamp or a telephone pole—that I had not seen. Had not seen but, still, could imagine, though probably wrongly, the face very clear but for no good reason—reason, as in sight. What this brought to mind, instead, was something equally missing: in moments, in the wrong season, among palms, while moving among the summer-shuttered houses, walking in an Ohio winter, trees impermanently bare except, perhaps, for catkins, and a hope born out of cold blue. And white breath. I say "hope" (for tonight, there seems to be an "I") without the slightest hope of finding the word I really mean—hope is as strangely fitted, as a cloak, to the breath of experience as the appearance of the woman, fitted, even in the imagination only, to her self.

21   HM

She is BOLD as toast on the outside today: Boldly, this woman crosses
the street against the light,

the hardest job in the world. Creak, creak & still she wears those super-

long silk three-tiered skirts like one she wore in the photo

when once she lived in
another world, one where, squatting in the simmering, wild foothill creek,

she pleased her mouth by eating pure wild-creek mint.

Distinctly, now, she is wearing out her heels (& knees) with a hard-hitting

heel-to-toe step/knee-high black leather, boots & that sweet bird's nest
at the back of her head, revealing an unwitting exposure in rest—

that nest un-nesting the skull beneath her

several shades of variations on the theme of dyed locks, where the roots of snow

& bone shine out from the under-world, white as a baby's dwarf-white

fingernails.

& the sky full

of incubating egg-shaped clouds. Yet

she is beautiful as a jade gossamer parachute, fur collar clinging like a monkey to

her

neck.

21 SM

They smell her. (Let's assume, for a time, that "she," in fact, exists.)

The four dogs bark themselves to the edge of the fenced-in yard:
one hundred crows fly north.

Looser than migration.

Into the white-tinged apricot of sky, its French trees butchered, clumped.

(*Curette*, the dental hygienist had said. *It's something I have to do*.)

Across the street, a drove of dwarves and pink flamingos. Several leprechauns.

To make the teeth like silk.

And plastic witch-hat Christmas trees, stranded in ornaments.

There's no escaping the leaf-blowers.

What is it to be very old?

(The white Continental, covered with a plastic tarp and bricks.)

To slowly walk, with one's slow dog.
To be, rightly, bewildered.

This is not a way to seduce, but seduction's overrated.

(In the sink, the clippings of the nails. Old cologne.)

22   HM

She finally arrived (after having been nearly forgotten), leaving

her reflection glancing off the rear-view mirror of the canary-yellow Chevy
Impala—
the impact of her image lingering & gradually demisting

the fogged-up windows, the chrome.
Every dawn came over the hill differently & although the hill seemed the same,
it wasn't,
it changed

at every glance of light, of sound & so
she escaped again & again,

& he did not seem either to notice, or somehow had persuaded himself
to ignore the fact of her freedom, her increasingly satin patina.

(No one knew the vehicle was unlocked & thus accessible from the right front
passenger side. It was easy to be distracted by the bumper stickers, which one
had to be very close to, to make out.)

He therefore could continue the ruse of the self with no self-accusations, no mirrors,
no blades. His hair began to fray & take on a life of its own. It had the steaming
scent of ore.

22   SM

She had learned to speak to the ones who were already dead,
or as though they could hear her.

She wanted to say how much the things that happened
were not like lace.

She would arrange the sentences afterwards,
at the end.

The names she had wanted to forget
were not the small ones.

"I'm sitting there," a man she'd known began each conversation,
as though sitting were the only normal thing to do.

She had begun to feel the edges
of her limits.

No amount of food could cover it.

The small connections of being
were beginning to slip.

Even vigilance did not prevent this.

She lit candles to remind her
of herself.

Her hands were full of fur.

23   HM

"Make my grave shallow so I can feel the rain"—
this is all stolen but "I" don't truly care—
all the moveable parts are mine now

&

when I come back, it will be as a
very tall woman wearing tight madras shorts,
& a filthy eggshell faux-fur coat.
"I'll" play the accordion (exceptionally well)
& maybe the mouth harp for driving
long distances midwinter, & a golden harp
for obvious reasons & times of service—"I'll"
sing with a mouth full of absolutely perfect teeth,
& "my" blood will arrange itself
like a well-set dinner table.

"I"

will be aching with sentences like,
"I" am what was & the bonfire of the ore-sewn sky,"
or "My name is John; therefore, no one listens"—
things like that & there will be no
more questioning whether there really is a "she"
or a "he" &

it

will have been completely forgiven (read *absorbed*).

23   SM

(It had been a rainbow of waves: indigo, azure, teal, aqua, turquoise, lavender and white. Maybe periwinkle.)

White towels, wadded on the stainless steel.
(Which had stained.)

Mr. Agenda straightens his tie.

Nothing, anymore, is warm.

(Derangement was about to be a national condition.

Therefore, the so-called "bake and reside."

Tense grew rather tense
and strained. Made no "sense.")

24 HM

What waltzed up the alley that night was root scent—
sea-foam, seaweed, the impermanent gray-stone of fog—
    easily colorlessly hidden
in omens which swooned between the hipster's blue-jeaned legs, those dancing
or simply swaying thus under the yellow rings of lamp light.

Jazz up, every musician in the roadway was   dressed in black   (of course),
with unusual sideburns, tattooed with old addresses, obscure   Taoist sayings—
lines known by heart, by the slim-hipped, nearly   nude women
pressed in a line up against the ancient brick wall,   their skin

simmering
like almonds & pearls,
the stalks of their arms,
their magical necks
tickling the air to the rhythm,
like Poseidon's messenger swans—

opening exactly in the way we want   music to split us open,
like extravagant sex—

the beat of the band undoing their legs, undoing, too, the gingered glances
sipping
at the fine white hairs on each half-undressed breast, as the velvet

darkness swallowed,
exhaled,
riding the long sideways swirled lines
of electric cello, undoing, too,

the tight chests of the long-haired men in cowboy boots, the Harley riders,
the lawyers & surfers, the painters & clingers,

while expensive modern furniture seemed to float over our heads, then
unwind tornadoesque into the canopy
of heaven
before whisking off into
the overhead freeway of grape(y) planetary mystery.

Next, what came were
two people who seemed to be one, a pair of brown men holding hands, a child haloed

in rainbow minnows,
three dogs licking
the pads of each other's paws,
then a wiped-out suit in a brand new car
all jittered & coifed for prowling
the swaying curves of hungry women

    & then the tap, tap of well-heeled ghosts   shivering & kissing
                                                        the mouths of the living
                                                        under the doe-wet watchful
eyes

of the enormous painted Aztec faces peering down from the sky with such
tender fatigue.
& me then at last, the parchment photo of a woman,
eyes the eyes of ashes—   not diffuse, but turning
                                                invisible,
                                                polished

beneath the Japanese bamboo that hush-hushed over the old redwood fence—
leaves like flocks of small cerulean birds   with wings of wind,

as the ends of my hair grasped the singing vowels slipped from the lips
of the waves breaking, breaking
on the hours of particle sand
half a mile away   & the light
                                                radiant from
                                                everything

amending my ribs (like cellos) back to the soil
& the "she" that "I" was was no longer
but always will be & I no longer wanted to be other than within all,
& without all & nothing more or less than   the unwinding
into
the night's   clockwork of smoke,
                                            the blankets of shadow—

those corner messages from God,   which sound

nearly exactly like, no really, exactly the same as

laughing.

24   SM

The man, you see, is expressing, is pressing his life right into the microphone. There are forty or fifty or maybe sixty or seventy watching him do this.

He is standing in front of a wall of lipstick-colored windows. No one can hear him.

Like a crowd—but no one can see it—there is a large murmuring growing in size from behind the windows.

No one emerges.

But the sound keeps increasing, the windows (really a kind of wax paper with serrated edges—you could probably tear them off the wall) are filling with sound, as though a whole building of lives, every life at once, like an ocean, full of its sound, invisible, swelling behind the glass and the colors of lipstick—

The sound of this wall is larger than amplification.

And the man, with his words, keeps talking like a movie with the sound off and it is *everybody's* story now that everyone listens to instead, even though we can't make out the words, can't see the bodies the story belongs to as it keeps advancing on the wall like the wind through a three-story cottonwood tree that blows all night with the joy of a vertical ocean—

and it's *all* the leaves we hear that make that sound.

25   HM

Such talk, such rabble
came up the hill from the dark & unquiet sea.

The water in her garden hose had not been warmed
for the three quarters of the year

behind them, was curled

in the yard like a slumbering stone cat. Next door, new people
had planted wild carnations, lettuce,

sunlight starved,

artichokes had breached the soil.
A big black dog stood near a black phone pole.

Nothing moved as she passed.

The scent once more—

broken rain, crushed cedar. She was almost

old, was dressed in two shades of blue—horizon, earth,

salmon skirts of dawn. She was walking. The umbrella
was not yet needed—would be.

Lifted, her face lulled as if it were drizzling against her windows at home

& she wanted wetness.

She remembered she'd dreamt of a bear,

then opened the umbrella just to hear its loft. North,
there was the harbor

& as suddenly, the kiss

she recalled just this once,

as if she were lying
in her bed at last breath, fingers still on her breast-bones &

sunlight over her ribbons of hair ruffling too

with song.

25   SM

So we went on the velvet journey of his voice.
And the girl, then, opened a brook.

He knew (well) how to apologize
for nothing.

And she, too, allowed the forehead lines
their natural shadow.

It was a private country that they made.

We followed it as long as there was sound.

And the mechanical caws crowing.

She had opened a brook.

And he had opened his private voice.

It was not, at that time, difficult to let go
of everything at night.

But where was the whipped architect(ure)
of the sheets?

There was simply no place to enter.

The words had been guarding her
from their experience.

Once the sound had stopped.

It had become chimerical.
A miracle.

It was about nothing.

And someone was going to misread that as "criminal."
Or shimmer.

Or camera.

The animals could smell no fear.

Process counted, we know.

Sometimes you just had to wait.

Terrible, I know.

To wait, that is, for yourself.

More terrible.

26

"It is deserted," she says.

"The house? Your body? When? When did it happen?" he says.

"Finally," she says & opens the door for him.

26   SM

(At the center of this was a dream about a man she could not remember (in an office she could not recall) who told her things she did not understand: the speech was garbled. She asked him to repeat what he'd said. It sounded exactly the same.)

27   HM

While going up she asks   the jowly man in

the elevator—*What's in the cooler?*   *Body parts*, he replies.

Which ones? She asks   *Two left hands & The " I," I mean*

an eye, the color of grass, no glass, an emerald rose.   But

chickens don't fly, she whispers, then does,

leaping out

from the penthouse, her nose parting air sleek as an undone bundle of cherry blooms, loosened by wind, by hot sun from the trees' limbs, her own skin like fine lingerie silking before exploding over the imploding city

streets humming like bees & lips moving without sounds, or was it

sound without meaning, meaning unstrung, but in a good way, or so

she thought later.

27   SM

Here is your mirror, because you can't see: how the quick-blossoming petals feel/fill the whole body as rosebuds explode in the breast, pressing, but gently, up into the flesh. Behind the knees we begin to see fire as they flutter against the inside of the forehead, ruffle the crevice surrounding your heart while the skin holds them in like a girdle, stretched smooth—oh body, oh sack full of roses—in the thrum of the belly, they thrive / they impinge on the skin of the sack of the scrotum and equally, fingers get tangled, abuzz, in plump petals—loud sweetness—they press to the soles of the feet.

Here is the falling that's really a flying. Here is the humming and churring of bees, corollas inviting a chorus of honey, a nest thin as ash—but not ash, not ash—until, when you look, you can no longer see your reflection:

the eyes—they are nothing but roses—

both "I"s in the mirror—unfolding, quick-blossoming roses of green.
My dear—can you see?—there is nothing to fling.

28

Twice now, she'd been blinded, but this time in the color blue.

His tenure with the layers of flowering plants became another skirt she wanted to wear & remove only under his hands. But there were problems—

the various sizes of the suspension bridges & what sang between the bridges for one—the infants & un-flung ashes for another. She listened, ear against his throat & lungs, which

were as large & full as

the big & small surf that laid the rhythm of the world's heart out before him like an open palm asking him, one small person, to ride over the sorrow, the blue waves into

the unwinding ball that is the sun.

Still, it lifted, the ruffled flute of her breath

(shanti)

& so, again

she considered planting the white seeds of the night garden. Fear would be one bright sweet bloom undone, opened & at rest—

since *the body can be ruined but not the flayed heart*

&, in the end, the stretched blue of the sea is the mirror & the

mirror is the unblinking eye.

28   SM

There was her method of swooning, which involved letting go on an ice rink of shattered glass, her long red hair strewn over the crackles, cheek bones against ice cube pebbles (in their sharpness, like a mirror) and the sense that below the ice glass or glass ice was another room that could be looked into, or looked up from. At around the same time, she noticed more men staring at her in the grocery store, where she had chosen recently to expose her eyes—and their wariness—their willingness, now, to assess and retract—a process she would allow the men to see as it occurred, and though she despised this—there was the recognition that her prior openness had limits—she saw, at the same time, their fascination, realized this as a part of the allure of women who had always seemed somehow "older" than she would ever be, more "knowing," even when they were young. It was an animal look—the look of someone interested in survival primarily—that she hadn't imagined, especially in moments of dismissal, could attract. But in those moments on the cold glass, her skin seemed even more pale and translucent—like something not meant to survive, impossible as protective cover—and the gaze of assessment was trained on her own face while her body—sinuous and arduously long, angular as a spider—lay in its mass of hair: puzzling, unforgettable.

29   HM

It's Thanksgiving & it's rained hard. Dust washed, the residual daylight slants from clouds near the sea, a mile off the sea, big mountain pulling & pulling our blood to its own long beating time.

Every dawn, an old Asian couple walks these streets, up the center—twin shadows threading through morning. Yet tonight they come at dusk, quiet feet in sync, passing as house after house burnishes up, people laying tables for gatherings & celebrations. Always before, the two slipped by in silence, but tonight, she is humming very softly.

Veiled in the plum-blue ending of day, I sit alone on the porch two doors down from my own, in a garden I built for this neighbor last spring. In my mind's eye, I see its geometry long after I'm gone, beyond that too—the visiting wrens, the dropped weight of white roses, lavender trumpet vines limp with fog. Meyer lemons punk & ripe: yellow lanterns, not harvested, heavy. Slow brown spiders hang between the limbs.

A young Welshman I've known claims he won't cut his hair, not ever again. He loves riding big waves more than his life. Tall body intent, deliberate nearly transparent with will—steady seed in the tunnel's core.

His young brother, once in from Wales, mused at this quiet LA—unexpected, distant from tales of gun wars, whores—the real battles & class conflicts zigzagging in the currents at the neighborhood's end. Bewildered,
nearly let down, he wondered at this peace, these rooms of peaceful gardens—

where, tonight, ruffles of cold settle over my face, as it too grows still, features
diminished, form disappearing at each curl of wind, until I am the breath in
& of itself—blood—a lamp, lungs & air drumming, steadfast as waves—
the ones he so loves, the thunder breaking & breaking with force against
the nearby shore. Dreaming the pulse, my body is pulled open by darkness until,
vaguely, I wonder why this month old lovers keep trying to find me, as if curious
to study the shape of things after so many years—how it all turned out so far.

A bat slices by. An odd bird sings twice. Beyond windows I see neighbors
begin breaking bread at tables lit with candles, scattered with flowers/
repeating the way it has been & will be for years, while the spell of night kneels
to tend each leaf, petal, fruit & branch, re-shaping the stones with ripe devotion—
the lover who loves past the body's strength, & beyond that too, into the deep
sapphire lake of everything that ever was—

like the silent couple who never touch, yet walk as one up the these nondescript
streets, up the center, just as darkness reveals the secrets of itself, opening
like a woman who trusts the comer/wants him to enter until each become,
for a moment, the other—the light of night, the shadows of day, as if all is
water falling, water falling, all is falling, & so becoming—forever,
again—nothing, once more.

29   SM

But there was another subject.
What was it?
It had been deserted by form—
by forms of all kinds.
One could say "river" or "bird" or "fish"
or even "ash"—
and it was none.
And had been none.
And so it was with some irony that this could be said/felt/thought
on a day that was "beautiful," if cold.
That rivery strands of water fell into a round, raised cement pool
like a river peeing—peeing from eight angles at once.
That a slim tree, the color of ash, was budding
as light hit the ash-grey deck through the greenery
gathered like flowing swords—gathered into
the vase of the earth/the face of the earth
with its many mouths.
Light hit the prayer flags like wind
or wind hit them like light.
But there were no fish.
No birds.
(And the man in the dream said,
*You'll just have to feel it
like it is.*)

30   HM

It happens when we're very tired.

We remember the lands, which now retreat to water,
going about slumber in basic increments, hazed as if in layers of heather.
There have been too many mirrors.

Because we love the men we love
we don't forget them,
their lips parted on our breasts,
seeds
in our mouths—each specific thing, quiet & true—
their voices lingering inside us

unavoidably waked by even something that may seem really
quite small—
what it is to be within the flame.

30   SM

Strands of sirens and crows: the whole world hauls itself awake. Clouds like a muddy curtain. Sodden ticking of blades, high above birds—a helicopter, its blinking light. The world not ready for day—a disruption—stones and terra cotta and flux—the deepening hue of the rain—a stem of water that runs like a long white tongue from the hose, recycling into a fountain—odd paean to water, contained, in a yard of wet and battered leaves so limp, so waterlogged, they sag to the ground like spent candelabras.

Even the gray cat wants to come in.

As if waking is nothing more than acknowledgement of loss.
Day coming on like a hangover, everything bright in its wreckage, too sated to rise, too spent, the crows all a-murder in early, reluctant construction. Their terrible voices: ripping, breaking the seal of dawn.

31   HM

Twisting, we smell of wet horses/salt/granite,

(like Christ), in the deep cup of winter
my body is the bridge.

I understand by making circles
against you in the darkness
with my white hips, & see too

all those thousands
of migrating monarchs in Santa Cruz
falling through the eucalyptus grove air/

falling in orange love to death/

*(I have known you always
is what the woman says with her body*

*& knows
& the man knows or
has forgotten or tries to forget)*

again, again,

the hundred or more butterflies,
breathless, in pairs
of black skeletal wings,

falling and still with love.

31   SM

—Mystery Box

What you cannot see is the black river,
how the horizon merges into sand, the sky goes granular—

and what might have begun as clouds,
hills.

Someone has the idea of an oarsman,
standing on a wooden raft,
ferrying a lounging man

and a shape, ambiguous—

from this angle, it looks like a dead horse
or a folded robe.

And the oar no bigger, really, than a needle,

dips into the idea of black, the water scored
like an old LP.

Someone has taken spring away,
and summer,
and water.

You cannot see the ants as they come at your
bare, bloody feet.

You look up
into the endless sand of sky.
There is no sky.

32   HM

I took you inside.
I took the vein & apple.
I took your stem & held & held.
I took the after & before.
I could not help it.

Bird in storm. Bird under cloud.
Bird.

And inside my cunt, these things arrived:
A bowl of sweet purple blood:
Ten thousand oaks.
Too many moons & pavilions to count.
White sand sifting from my womb like sugar—
your murdered father,
the blue rings on his neck,
on my own,
the lands of grass & those,
those tall standing stones,
huge as men who can see the
black lake so fragile it's invisible
as air & yet it's tumbling with birds,
who sing the
dream where you tell me
I'm not too old.
That it doesn't matter.
It's not too late (did you *speak?*)
This land has no law.

32 SM

The dark space was now in a hollow—a sort of gully—rather than a spike

as though she carried it around in a purse

except inside herself—maybe the gully was located somewhere

in the chest (she had confused hyena with pariah or

they should have been confused)

and it would be interesting to know

("there was only one hate on top of the table")

if this was what they called, officially

("in a serious of jumbled thoughts")

"depression"—or just a bunch of masks on the page

(lifting the hem of the photograph's gown).

(I meant "marks.")

33   HM

There was no handbook. We shook—sometimes all over in fear (even when there were veils of stratus clouds or fog which from below were much as they were from above & we understood this but could not fly). In mirrors

our bodies grew strange, teeth stratus, joints stalagtites & transparent opal ropes tethered to each lovely chime of bone—muscles, roots, our piece of the mangrove grove.

& for a time I was joined specifically with one quite thin man, after which my body was temporarily misplaced, like a cloud.
I saw that I loved him for some reason of the body & would always &

he sent me a note in the ethers from the ethers, which was also the sapphire curve of the big wave—it said, "Unus Mundus"—which deserved only
the "Yes" (like a pearl),

the word every woman knows because she remembers that she speaks moon.

33   SM

If it occurs in a room, the room is white—sheer white—
and if someone walks there, the movement is purple

—almost a shadow, but sheerer.

One drop of color.
The spine

—hung like loose hose
in its socket.

Night.

Tablet of light
on a table

like a narrow moon.

And there are the fake footsteps again. A door closing.

Or someone is humming: just two notes—a step.

No.

Not like a moon,
like a tablet.

Punctual as a clock.

And there is melody, repeating.
Repeating, not progressing.

Someone is whistling, or is it a bright
instrument.

A window with no edges.
Only suggestions of edges

that continue to move.
Further away than a moon.

34   HM

There are changes in her features. The skin is poor but the voice is, as always, seductive. Some can't help being so hungry, black thoughts, follow pinpricks & principles, the tenacious ones—follow, too, like a small pack of dirtied poodles, muzzled, but stout-hearted & sniffing for the goods, especially when a full moon comes, oozing out a carpet of pearls she might sleep upon while it flies over the cities of the world. In every moment she steps into a hole & out & in & out. There are other whips too.

She knows they can smell the damp, murky wetness emanating from her spine, changing the air near her neck & head as if she is wearing a hat of snakes or leaves. Peering, first fiercely, then shallowly from behind the onion of her skin cave, she never forgets. How would it be to swallow a man's leg, just getting to his cock? Such is the image of the snake's hunger & Eve's abandonment by love with a capital letter. Spinning around every corrosion, all these weather veins standing upright again—would that get her a new resume? Would she be restored her crown of stars? Even as she tips like a faulty three-masted ship, you ask if she'd be able to describe it,

say, as just trying to tie herself like a wind-up doll to her hips with a double-barreled flask so she could get through the journey. Love would have directed her better had love been better able to Love. Her skirts need hitching up, are dragging in the wave breaks. The sunlight makes a cool landing, while she keeps trying to fly by flapping her arms & lining her lips coral, having filled things in with small tattoos of x's & o's—as if this would get her up, up, up enough, would speed the momentum she needs for take-off.

34 SM

—November, After the Jeffers Fest

There was the way the sea felt at night,
which was the way it looked—

black, the streetlamps making a cold
brightness. Damp. The emptying

crowds, a sparseness—air
between palms, the open

unwelcoming.

In the lit room of memory,
so densely alive

      (the deer, that they are here . . .)

roses, sisters of the sycamore, the owl—

nothing like the billboards of thin
eternity.

The great-horned, 28, alert,
blinking above a falconer's glove—

though, with its glass bones, it cannot fly.

A squadron of roses carving their nods of deep peach
into air, like a chorus.

Those two trees behind them, leaves like split hearts,
fastened to the ground.   Transacting.

Impossible not to feel them.

And to the left, my friends—Brendan, in his bug-eyed
shades; Cathie, in her shawl—

my friends, who have become themselves, also.

And even I—I, who had abandoned
all notion of miracle—

35   HM

The brightness of March daffodils shook his nervous system. Rarer,
the soft mat of what gradually became love—loomed
of a certain darkness, sweetish mossness,
the sort of place where wrecked cars lay like animal skeletons
disseminating the tree canopy as if reciting music as they rusted
into mud & for them no other spring return.
He had left his footprints in the sand
& somehow they'd stayed on her bedding.
He left a formal greeting in the tealeaves
in six languages & she understood each
as a portion of the water she sipped from a glass bowl.
Water, clean & cold,   made of a river.
Water, clean & cold,   made of snow.
He was without a mother & wife always.
She had many moons ago slipped into his windows,
had been cleaning the dust from the picture frames, the interior images
so he could see what past, what future meant.
There was a lot more rain than either might have presumed.
& she washed first her hair in it,
& then his before they slept hipbone to hipbone.
They stayed like this for hours.

35 SM

If the presence in the hallway

        Turned out to be music,

It was more like shadow—

        As a boy silently exploring

A foreign hotel

        Middle of noon

A kind of night—

        That quiet, private

Stifling

        The corridor, long and weirdly still

(As if all drapes are made of velvet)

        An orchestra playing the one secret chord

(A small tapping, wavering, slight

        As a twig almost hitting a window

Repeatedly, in shadow,

        Not sound, but the small repeated movement

One could make out in the window shade

        Or pale, gathering drops of rain—

Their silhouette and huddle

        How their presence barely arises,

Registers as visible—)

        That may, in fact, be memory

Or some other pattern

        Shifting, nearly imperceptibly,

In the mind

        As the coughing begins again

And a woman in the theatre

        Leaves her seat, trying to muffle

The sound

        In her chest

There is a looseness

        Trying to get loose

Whispering

        To the young man taking tickets in the lobby

Do you have some water?

36   HM

(Waltz)

I am dancing, not quite falling—
the hours, made of whistles.

Things disappear, if not real.
Or if not made real. Or are left unmade—

beautiful empty cups like a red blur
of lit lanterns—what comes by chance or luck.

& how disturbing at times, just the voices of
strangers rising smoky as they walk the city.

Some facts revisit us—the kaleidoscope
faces of the lost ones
like torn shadows.

These are my arms, the twin white doves
of my hands opening, closing
as if weaving the wind.

Night has shown itself to be exactly itself
& secrets are always like hungry ghosts, like clouds.

The cold breeze at my neck is fitted as a dress—
Yet, I'm nowhere near finished,

love the scent of sharp things, the sting
of sun-baked eucalyptus broken
free in the late, late hours.

Once I saw a migration of snow geese.
& every single motion

was silent. Thousands flew so close to my body

I knew then I was falling.

36   SM

Necessaire: albedo. The white, bouncing light. Necessary: snow. In large patches. What had been forgotten: it is every hue. Now that the happy ending had been abandoned, we could re-enter the room. Every hue was present. Every part of light. What is purity anyway, but a moment? Maybe this one.

This one, beyond the strictures of white—of white misconstrued, misunderstood, of white reduced to paint instead of crystal, to something opaque, flattened beyond the turning point.

Every hue is welcome.
This one, the moment after giving up all hope

—all projection. So that the light can project
onto you.

37   HM

Maybe it was snow he dreamed of—the man standing in front of the mirror
midday with his body slick & wet. Maybe it was his wife—a mountain
without hunger, his coarse hair black again & his arm, an old tree under her
river, body returned to the certainty of a master cellist sitting in a field,
playing undisturbed, not holding anything back—from the water, the clouds,
the splitting perfumed air.

In the dream, he cannot conceive anything is ever really lost—exactly
the same way that, beyond the open bathroom window, he has for years
watched a women grow old alone, yet she too is rare with white clouds,
coins of pure motion—not forgetting, not forgotten.

Maybe it was rice in the dream, filling every cup & running mouth, hunger
unadorned, as a current of water fell over his body, then through his fingers
in white crisp kernels (like snow), but he was not cold or afraid, simply curious,
looking closely at his own blurring form made of bone, all the while listening
to his daughter in her room, playing her oiled violin, on strings of splintering
wood—making her music, her hunger.

In the annotation of the mirror, he sees his mother, unraveled as a bandage
or a package—she is carrying an unearthed vessel of snow white rice
from the emerald rows of paddies, & now he is made of steam, his own shadow
passing over his face on the shower glass, his dog sleeping somewhere, quivering
in a world full of planes & cars & old women in their kitchens washing stones—
in the glass, he watches his mother melt a white drift of ice over his skin, before

his wife uncovers years, hours of scars, unwrapping him tenderly, tenderly
laying his frozen limbs with dogwood petals & strange names before re-sewing
his muscle to skin. His wife hums in the other room as he stands near the open
window (the old woman is naked & sleeping, standing at her sink) &

like a mountain, he somehow manages to reach up. He raises a field of fog.
What did she breathe into his mouth—under him in the dark when he was
the future? The crone? His wife? *Don't forget the winter.* He can't recall any song
that is not somehow full of snow. Her voice tumbles under the whistle
of the glass kettle in the kitchen (the old woman, the window, her folded hands).
The oil on his hand imprints his face with an abacus of lines, of unwritten music.
& he does then remember—

the cherry trees, their impermanence, the pearled & forgetful sweetness
of them—lifting in spring. And such a light, those tiny flowers flying,
whirling in exactly the same shade of pink as her nipples. The rice is like rain
now or petal buds, or humming, or steam, or a kiss, or a roof heavy with snow.
He remembers the color of the blossoms undoing themselves & leaping into
the air & how, once, no one was hungry or he'd just forgotten hunger
& they had always been singing & their naked feet in the silver snaked rivers
of grass were fully healed.

37

It was just a field—
but that night it was *the meadow*,
and it glowed—

like nothing else around it glowed.

I walked down the hallway of my parents' house
to the kitchen,
to be sure—

sure that no light source
explained this.

There had been the long, shrill call
of an animal—a sweet call—

one I'd never, before, heard.

In the way that coyotes sometimes wake us
in the thick of night—

the sound of a crane.

Or two. The sound of two.

In their shrill, sweet, unexpected vocal dance
of mating.

Or of calling. Maybe just of calling.

In their inability—having heard the other call—
to sustain their silence.

In their recognition of each other—
before even seeing.

In their shared tone.

Which was more remarkable—the calling,
or the glow?

Or was the meadow calling to the cranes

—whose call slipped back into the night,
a disappearing carving.

By morning, the field was
once again a field.

But then just a few days later, far above the path
that led into a small municipal park

of blackberries and uncut grass, of maple and madrona—

like a river of velvet rowers

crossing the large sky—

the sound of their wings so different from the sound of their cry—

entirely another color—

crossing the large water of air, the large water of the sky

in a gray whir, a gray embrace of velvet flapping—

were scores of black crows,

leaving behind their gargoyle perches on condo rooftops

and settling in small flocks within their larger Concordia—

black-frocked choirs, silent, settled

in the tops of trees—

like onyx magnolias

suddenly sprung at the end of summer, in the pink heat—

twenty-five or thirty at a time.

And there had been the finest white silk thread of hair

at 40,000 feet—the clouds twirling over, under, through

themselves as though they were, themselves, the motion

of an orchestrated score against uninterrupted cobalt—

suspended in, against the backdrop of that pure blue

  which should have no weight, is endless,

  which must have some texture we can feel as blue,

  without even looking;

  which must be, itself, some kind of light;

which refuses, in this moment,

to declare itself as blank

—or less than fully tangible—

and the flight of white and slow and crystal music curled

in its lengthening embrace of shifting feathering across the stone—

that stone also suspended

there, that cuticle of moon.

Because it was all I could do to keep from screaming,

right there, on the plane,

I knew it was beautiful.

If this was a prayer, my entire body could hear it.

It was as though my whole body was an eye.

It would be important, I knew, to find a way to say this simply.

To try.

NOTES

The opening epigraph is from John Rewald's *The Impressionist Brush*, in a passage describing Renoir's *Nude in the Sun*.

1 SM—"Practices and habits" is the lingo of Thanissaro Bhikkhu, of Metta Forest Monastery (www.dhammatalks.org).

3 HM—Robert Graham's towering bronze *Retrospective Column* (1981, cast in 1986) is part of the permanent collection at LACMA.

4 HM—Thank you, Beatles, for "I am The Walrus" & "Here Comes the Sun."

5 SM—Thank you, Edward Hopper.

15 HM—"The Sleeping Gypsy," 1897, by Henri Rousseau, is on view at MOMA, NYC.

17 HM—The practice of "Doodlebugging" or " Water Witching" is the process of using a form of divination, usually using a simple tool (dowsing rod or pendulum), in order to locate sources of underground water. www.dowsingworks.com

16 SM—The Freud in question is Lucien, though the other one, as always, hovers.

23 HM—"Make my grave shallow so I can feel the rain" is a quotation from the opening of the Dave Mathews song "Gravedigger" (also performed by Willie Nelson).

29 HM—"The breath in & of itself"—language taken from Thanissaro Bhikkhu of Metta Forest Monestary (www.dhammatalks.org)

34 SM—*"The deer, that they are here"* has in mind George Oppen's "The wild deer bedding down / That they are there!" from his poem "Psalm." "Glass bones" in owls (a condition much like rickets in humans) is caused by a lack of organ meats in the diet: the bones would break if the owl attempted flying.

36 SM—"Come. Be gentian, emerald. Any color in light." –Stephany Prodromides

HD and Bergman also lurk here, like breath, especially *Trilogy*, *The Silence*, and *Persona*. So does the *qasida*, as a form. Herzog's *Cave of Forgotten Dreams* and Moby's *Destroyed* were tonics for re-entering. Later, so was Massive Attack's "Paradise Circus" with Hope Sandoval. Later, Beethoven: Opus 133. Later, *Abbey Road*.

Thank you, Alice Fulton, for this: " . . . a painting is not an illustration / but a levitation, dense / as mind . . ." (from *Felt*).

ACKNOWLEDGEMENTS

Our deepest gratitude to the editors and publishers of the following publications—with special thanks for your encouragement, curiosity, courage, and interest in collaborations—in which many of these poems first appeared, sometimes in different versions or with different designating numbers or titles.

HM: *Askew, Bizy Buti, La Fovea, The Laurel Review, Mentalshoes, The Offending Adam, Poemeleon, Parthenon West Review*

SM: *Askew, The California Journal of Poetics, Chaparral, FIELD, La Fovea, The Laurel Review, Mentalshoes, The Offending Adam, Ocho 23, Pedestal, Poemeleon, Spillway, Superstition Review, The Taos Journal of Poetry & Art, Tupelo Quarterly, Zocalo Public Square*

More gratitude:

HM: Thank you is too small a saying to hold the reality of what my community of friends & colleagues have given. Nor can I name everyone here so please know that everything & everyone I have ever known with any depth has given to the making of the work as it is with life and art. But I must name a few—Dr. Erna Osterweil, who has saved my mind from the hell realms, Lilly Dale Reed, Sudie Shipman, Celeste Goyer, Laura Amazzone, Christine Lopez, Alan Davis, River Mary Malcolm, Christine Downing, Judith Pacht, Katherine Williams, Richard Garcia, and . . .

HM & SM: . . . and those we have to thank jointly, hugely, for their contributions to our process in making this, and for the way they have shaped our vision and drawn it into the aural world:

to David St. John, for early belief in this project, enduring encouragement, and for egging us on, and to James Cushing, Jeffrey Levine, Richard Mathews, and Gail Wronsky, for generous and unstinting responses that were essential in helping us find the final shape of the manuscript . . .

and to Marjorie Becker, Jeanette Clough, Dina Hardy, Paul Lieber, Jim Natal, Jan Wesley, Brenda Yates, Mariano Zaro; Sandra Alcosser, Ralph Angel, Brendan Constantine, Marsha De La O, Anne Fisher Wirth, Beckian Fritz Goldberg, Veronica Golos, Robert Hass, C. D. Wright, Louise Mathias, Holly Prado and Harry Northup, Chuck Rosenthal, Cathie Sandstrom, Phil Taggart, Lynne Thompson, Cecilia Woloch; Fred Dewey, Marci Vogel, Karen Kevorkian, Maureen Alsop, Cati Porter, David Dodd Lee, Tess Lotta, Stephany Prodromides, Barbara Blatt, Hilda Weiss and Wayne Lindberg, Richard Modiano and Carlye Archibeque, Bill Mohr, Cathie Strisik, Chad and Jennifer Sweeney, Nik de Dominic, Andrew Wessels, Angie Estes, Kathy Fagan Grandinetti, John Gallaher, Frank Giampetro, David Young, David Walker, Jamie Hazlitt, Kristine Bracolini, Albert Hickman, and Elena Karina Byrne.

SM: Additional thanks to some folks who created a climate of inspiration particular to these poems, and who may not realize it: Arthur Kell, Daniel Tiffany, Elizabeth Willis, Jessica Fisher, Peter Eirich, Molly Bendall, Marlena Dali and the Kate Crash Band, Suzanne Lummis, M.L. Colby, Bill Hogeland, Franz Wright, Aaron Reed, Linda and Miguel Sandoval, Timothy B. McCaffrey, Phil Cousineau, and my parents, Mary and Bruce Maclay.

And thank you to Jeffrey Wilson and Bellarmine College, Loyola Marymount University, for a writing retreat at the Immaculate Heart Center for Spiritual Renewal in Montecito, which allowed the focus required to begin to see this project as a whole.

***

We are so grateful to and inspired by everyone at What Books Press!

HOLADAY MASON is the author of *The Red Bowl* (Red Hen Press, 2016), *Towards the Forest* (2007) & *Dissolve* (2011), both from New River Press, University of Minnesota, as well as two chapbooks. Her manuscript *The Weaver's Body* was finalist & won honorable mention for the 2014 Dorset Prize & her chapbook "Transparency" was a finalist for the Snowbound 2015. Twice a Pushcart nominee, publications include *Poetry International, American Literary Review, Pool, Smartish Pace, Runes, Solo, The River Styx, The Spoon River Review,* and *The Laurel Review.* Co-editor of *Echo 681*, poetry editor of *Mentalshoes*.com, she is also a fine art photographer & has been a psychotherapist in private practice since 1996. www.holadaymason.com

SARAH MACLAY is the author of *Music for the Black Room* (2011), *The White Bride* (2008) and *Whore* (2004), all from U of Tampa Press, as well as three chapbooks. A 2015-2016 COLA Fellow and the recipient of a residency at Yaddo, her honors include a Pushcart Special Mention and the Tampa Review Prize for Poetry. Her poems and criticism have appeared in *The American Poetry Review,* T*he Writer's Chronicle, FIELD, The Best American Erotic Poetry: From 1800 to the Present, Ploughshares, Poetry International,* where she's served for more than a decade as Book Review Editor, and many other spots. A native of Montana and a graduate of Oberlin College and VCFA, she lives in Venice, California, teaches poetry and creative writing at LMU, and conducts Mini-Master Classes at Beyond Baroque.

LOS ANGELES

TITLES FROM
WHAT BOOKS PRESS

POETRY

Molly Bendall & Gail Wronsky, *Bling & Fringe (The L.A. Poems)*

Laurie Blauner, *It Looks Worse Than I Am*

Kevin Cantwell, *One of Those Russian Novels*

Ramón García, *Other Countries*

Karen Kevorkian, *Lizard Dream*

Holaday Mason & Sarah Maclay, *The "She" Series: A Venice Correspondence*

Carolie Parker, *Mirage Industry*

Patty Seyburn, *Perfecta*

Judith Taylor, *Sex Libris*

Lynne Thompson, *Start with a Small Guitar*

Gail Wronsky, *So Quick Bright Things*
BILINGUAL, SPANISH TRANSLATED BY ALICIA PARTNOY

ART

Gronk, *A Giant Claw*
BILINGUAL, SPANISH

Chuck Rosenthal, Gail Wronsky & Gronk,
Tomorrow You'll Be One of Us: Sci Fi Poems

PROSE

Rebbecca Brown, *They Become Her*

François Camoin, *April, May, and So On*

A.W. DeAnnuntis, *Master Siger's Dream*

A.W. DeAnnuntis, *The Final Death of Rock and Roll and Other Stories*

A.W. DeAnnuntis, *The Mermaid at the Americana Arms Motel*

A.W. DeAnnuntis, *The Mysterious Islands and Other Stories*

Katharine Haake, *The Origin of Stars and Other Stories*

Katharine Haake, *The Time of Quarantine*

Mona Houghton, *Frottage & Even As We Speak: Two Novellas*

Rich Ives, *The Balloon Containing the Water Containing the Narrative Begins Leaking*

Rod Val Moore, *Brittle Star*

Annette Leddy, *Earth Still*

Chuck Rosenthal, *Are We Not There Yet? Travels in Nepal, North India, and Bhutan*

Chuck Rosenthal, *Coyote O'Donohughe's History of Texas*

Chuck Rosenthal, *West of Eden: A Life in 21st Century Los Angeles*

Chuck Rosenthal & Gail Wronsky, *The Shortest Fairwells are the Best*

What Books Press books may be ordered from:
SPDBOOKS.ORG | ORDERS@SPDBOOKS.ORG | (800) 869 7553 | AMAZON.COM

Visit our website at
WHATBOOKSPRESS.COM

www.ingramcontent.com/pod-product-compliance
Lightning Source LLC
Chambersburg PA
CBHW020617300426
44113CB00007B/684